God Answers Prayer!

God Answers Prayer!

Ann Marie Lovejoy Bruce-Kerr

SUNESIS MINISTRIES

Copyright © 2024 Ann Marie Lovejoy Bruce-Kerr. The right of Ann Marie Lovejoy Bruce-Kerr to be identified as author of this work has been asserted by her in accordance with the Copyright, Designs, and Patents Act 1988. No part of this publication may be reproduced or transmitted in any form or by any means, electronic or mechanical, including photocopy, recording, or any information storage and retrieval system, without permission in writing from the author. Published by Sunesis Ministries.

For more information about Sunesis Ministries, please visit:

www.stuartpattico.com

ISBN: 978-1-0687248-0-0

The author of this book does not dispense medical advice or prescribe the use of any technique as a form of treatment for physical, emotional, or medical problems without the advice of a physician, either directly or indirectly. The intent of the author is only to offer information of a general nature. In the event you use any of the information in this book for yourself, the author and publisher assume no responsibility for your actions. The views expressed in this book are solely those of the author and do not necessarily reflect the views of the publisher, and the publisher hereby disclaims any responsibility for them. Scripture quotations marked "NKJV" are from the Holy Bible, New King James Version Copyright © 1982 Thomas Nelson, Inc. Used by permission. All rights reserved. Scripture quotations marked "KJV" are taken from The Holy Bible, King James Version. Scripture quotations marked "NIV" are taken from The Holy Bible, New International Version ® (Anglicised) Copyright © 1979, 1984, 2011 by Biblica, Inc. Used with permission. All rights reserved worldwide. Scripture quotations marked "ESV" are from The ESV® Bible (The Holy Bible, English Standard Version®), © 2001 by Crossway, a publishing ministry of Good News Publishers. Used by permission. All rights reserved. Scripture quotations marked (NLT) are taken from the Holy Bible, New Living Translation, copyright © 1996, 2004, 2015 by Tyndale House Foundation. Used by permission of Tyndale House Publishers, Inc., Carol Stream, Illinois 60188. All rights reserved. Scripture quotations marked "Amplified Bible" are taken from the Amplified® Bible (AMPC), Copyright © 1954, 1958, 1962, 1964, 1965, 1987 by The Lockman Foundation Used by permission. lockman.org.

.

Contents

Understanding Prayer	8
The Secret Place	13
Jesus' Pattern for Prayer	17
Praying with Authority	22
The Holy Spirit and Prayer	26
Types of Prayer	32
Prayer	42
Answered Prayer	46
Prayers you can use to pray	52
Answered Prayer record log pages	57

This book is dedicated to the loving memory of my Mum and Dad, who taught me so many life lessons; also, for my children David and Hannah, who are a gift to me from God.

1

Understanding Prayer

From a very early age I learnt what prayer was and the power of it. As a child I would have nightly visits from demonic spirits that would ask me to join them and disturb my peace. I was petrified but I knew instinctively that if I made the sign of the cross and asked God to help me, they would go away! As soon as I said, 'In the name of the Father, the Son and the Holy Spirit,' those things would scatter! I was a child of six years of age when I learnt to pray. I now pray with understanding and authority in my walk of faith with Christ. I pray and I see God move, as can you.

Prayer is a powerful concept that we as believers can yield at any given moment of the day, or any point in our life. It is literally communicating directly to our heavenly Father. What is wonderful about God is that He will hear you and cause you to triumph.

For us to enter into the kingdom of God, it starts with a simple prayer of faith. It is asking Christ to come into our heart, acknowledging Him as Lord and Saviour and asking Him to forgive us. God will hear you, speak to Him where you are at. He does not want pomp and ceremony; He just wants you!

Speak to Him from your heart, the bible tells us that God does not look at us from an outward appearance but, by what is in our heart:

'…….. For the Lord sees not as man sees: man looks on the outward appearance, but the Lord looks on the heart' (1 Samuel 16:7 NKJV)

In order to have an understanding of what prayer is, we must be in relationship with God. Prayer for a believer is not just an activity, saying wishy-washy words with no substance, nor is it an obligation, or begging God to tick off our wish list of what we want. It is communion and communication directly with Him that touches His heart. When you know what prayer is, you will begin to converse with God with adoration for His endless love for you, His grace and confidence He will impart to you.

The bible tells us that the earnest (heartfelt, continued) prayer of a righteous man makes tremendous power available (dynamic in its working) (James 5:16 Amplified Bible). Every prayer uttered from a believer's mouth based on God's word is heard by God. He will answer as soon as we ask.

Jesus told his disciples that 'they should always pray and not give up' (Luke 18:1). Jesus expected His prayers to be heard; He said, "Father, I thank you that you have heard me. I knew that you always hear me …" (John 11:41–42 NIV).

So, through Jesus' example, when we pray, we must have faith to know our prayers will be answered.

When we learn to pray in true faith, it will help us build a uniquely intimate relationship with God. It will cause us to love Him deeply, respect and revere Him, deepen our faith in Him, cause us to trust and stand upon His word and to have purpose and walk in it.

Someone once said that prayer is the expression of the human heart in conversation with God. It does take effort and commitment. When we pray, we are offering ourselves to God, releasing our desires and burdens, and surrendering our minds to Him.

When we pray it is a two-way conversation, it is not just making known what we want to happen, but also listening to God's response and being still in His presence, which can be healing in itself.We can find peace in prayer. We are reminded of this in I Peter 5:7 'casting all your care upon Him ......' Also, John 14:27 informs us: "Peace I leave with you, it is my own peace that I give you, I do not give it as the world does ...."

When we pray, there is not only a spiritual exchange, but an emotional one as well. If we allow Him, when we spend time in His presence, He will saturate our soul to the very core and heal and harmonise our emotions. God is interested in all that pertains to us and by giving God the legitimate right to intervene in earth's affairs as well as our own personal affairs, this will bring much peace and wisdom to our lives. The bible has plenty to tell us on this matter. Let's take a look at some scriptures:

> "If my people, who are called by my name, will humble themselves and pray and seek my face and turn from their wicked ways, then will I hear from heaven and will forgive their sin and will heal their land." (2 Chron. 7:14 KJV)

> "Let your reasonableness be known to everyone. The Lord is at hand; do not be anxious about anything, but in everything by prayer and supplication with thanksgiving let your requests be made known to God. And the peace of God, which surpasses all understanding, will guard your hearts and your minds in Christ Jesus." (Philippians 4:5-7

ESV)

'And pray in the Spirit on all occasions with all kinds of prayers and requests. With this in mind, be alert and always keep on praying for all the saints.' (Eph. 6:17-18 NKJV)

'Continue steadfastly in prayer, being watchful in it with thanksgiving.' (Col 4:2 ESV)

'Be joyful always; pray continually without ceasing; give thanks in all circumstances, for this is God's will for you in Christ Jesus.' (1 Thess. 5:16- 19 ESV)'Therefore I tell you, whatever you ask in prayer, believe that you have received it, and it will be yours.' (Mark 11:24 NIV)

There are a total of 367 scriptures in the bible that speak about prayer. Prayer allows us to enter into His presence behind the veil, into the Holy of Holies! It is our entry point into the spiritual realm to communicate directly with God and also for us to exercise our God-given authority through Jesus Christ against the enemy. When we begin to pray, we open up a portal into the spiritual realm to communicate directly to God.

Pray this prayer.....

Heavenly Father I come humbly before you and ask you to speak to me as I learn to speak to you, open my ears to hear you, open my eyes to see you and open my heart to receive your love. I ask this in the Name of Jesus, your Son. Thank you. Amen.

God Answers Prayer

2

The Secret Place

God has a secret place for each of us. How amazing is that! When we spend time with Him we will always be in that secret place; even when we are going about our everyday lives we stay connected to Him. We all need to rest and take time to recharge and regroup and where better a place to do this than in His presence, in that secret place where you commune with God Almighty and He can hear you and soothe your soul.

In the book of Psalms, it talks of dwelling in the secret place. The Hebrew word, "ba-se-ter" translated "secret place", appears only seven times in the Old Testament, five of which are in the Psalms. Along with "secret place" is also translated, "hidden part", "hidden place", "shelter" and "covert", in other scriptures. So, God's "secret place" is a hidden shelter His people can resort to and retreat into.

Psalm 91 tells us what we can expect in that secret place when we are safely there:

'Whoever dwells in the shelter of the Most High

will rest in the shadow of the Almighty.
I will say of the Lord, "He is my refuge and my fortress,
my God, in whom I trust."
Surely He will save you
from the fowler's snare
and from the deadly pestilence.
He will cover you with his feathers,
and under his wings you will find refuge;
His faithfulness will be your shield and rampart.
You will not fear the terror of night,
nor the arrow that flies by day,
nor the pestilence that stalks in the darkness,
nor the plague that destroys at midday.
A thousand may fall at your side,
ten thousand at your right hand, but it will not come near you.
You will only observe with your eyes
and see the punishment of the wicked.
If you say, "The Lord is my refuge,"
and you make the Most High your dwelling,
no harm will overtake you,
no disaster will come near your tent.
For He will command his angels concerning you
to guard you in all your ways;
they will lift you up in their hands,
so that you will not strike your foot against a stone.
You will tread on the lion and the cobra;
you will trample the great lion and the serpent.
"Because He loves me," says the Lord, "I will rescue him;
I will protect him, for He acknowledges my name. He will call on me, and I will answer him;
I will be with him in trouble,

The Secret Place

I will deliver him and honour him
With long life I will satisfy him
and show him my salvation." '
(Psalm 91 ESV)

When we dwell in the "secret place," we have the assurance that God is very close – so close in fact, that His shadow is falling over us.

This is the best place to be and the most secure place in which to abide. Here, you have direct communion with God, your private meeting place, exclusively where you meet Him and He meets you. It is where your love relationship with Him develops, your spiritual gifts develop, you find your deepest fulfilment.

In your secret place you share your all with your Creator; you share your dreams and your innermost secrets with God. It is that ultra-special "place" where you can get to know Him and where you can receive special instruction from Him for your life and what He will have you do for Him, for His kingdom's sake.

In the secret place, our spiritual person is nurtured and developed by Him. It is our holy place that He has allowed each of us to access by His grace.

In the book of Hebrews, it tells us to enter the throne room, the holy place, our secret place with God:

'Let us therefore come boldly unto the throne of grace, that we may obtain mercy, and find grace to help in time of need.' (Hebrews 4:16 KJV)

Pray this prayer .....

God Answers Prayer

Heavenly Father, hide me in the secret place so I can learn from you, commune with you and truly know you and walk with you in total victory over every area of my life. Amen

3

Jesus' Pattern for Prayer

Jesus frequently sought the Lord by himself, to enter into His secret place with the Father. He exemplifies this throughout the scriptures:

> 'And when He had sent them away, He departed into a mountain to pray.' (Mark 6:46 KJV)

> 'And he withdrew himself into the wilderness, and prayed.' (Luke 5:16 KJV)

Jesus spent much time in prayer as He wanted to find out what the Father's will for Him. He wanted to abide in the Father, so He could bring glory to God and bear much fruit (John 15:7-8 KJV).

He wanted to do the Father's will (John 5:30 KJV).

He wanted to find out what pleased the Father (John 8:29 KJV).

He wanted to speak the words of the Father (John 14:10 KJV).

Jesus provides the best example to follow for a divine prayer pattern.

One day Jesus was praying in a certain place. When he had finished, one of his disciples asked him to teach them to pray. Jesus then told them what we commonly known as the Lord's Prayer.

The Lord's Prayer should be understood as a pattern of how to pray. It is not just something to be recited as words; it was not intended to be used like that. It gives us the key ingredients that should go into prayer.

I am going to break it down for you so it can be something you base your prayers on when you talk to your heavenly Father.

Our Father who art in heaven

Begin your prayer with adoration to God. Praise Him for who He is and what He has done for you. The bible tells us that God *'inhabits the praises of His people'* (Psalm 22:3 KJV).

Hallowed be your name

Pray with adoration and reverence to God for who He is. Quote scripture in your prayer-time, like this beautiful scripture:

'There is none like you O Lord. You are great, and great is your name in might.' (Jeremiah 10:6 NKJV).

Thy kingdom come

Pray for more of God's presence on the Earth. Pray acknowledging that God is sovereign over your life and you want more of

Jesus' Pattern for Prayer

His kingdom manifest here on earth and in you:

> "Do not be afraid, little flock, for your father has been pleased to give you the kingdom." (Luke 12:32 KJV)

Thy will be done

Pray for God's will to be done, His plan for your life. Pray fully submitting your will and desires and trusting He will lead you:

> "For I know the plans I have for you," declares the Lord, "plans to prosper you and not to harm you, plans to give you a hope and a future." (Jeremiah 29:11 KJV)

Give us this day our daily bread

Pray believing and declaring God's provision in your life:

> 'Do not be anxious about anything, but in every situation, by prayer and petition, with thanksgiving, present your requests to God. And the peace of God, which transcends all understanding, will guard your hearts and your minds in Christ Jesus.' (Philippians 4:6-7 NIV)

Forgive us our debts

Pray confessing your sins to God, your heavenly Father and repent, turning away from those things that can cause us to stumble and fall. We have confidence knowing that the Lord is just and faithful to forgive us:

> 'If we confess our sins, he is faithful and just to forgive us our sins and to cleanse us from all unrighteousness.' (1 John1:9 NIV)

As we have also forgiven our debtors

Pray to forgive others. If we want our prayers heard we must forgive those who offend us. God understands that this is hard, but through prayer He can heal us and renew us so we are able to live a whole life, walking in the love of Christ:

> "Do not judge, and you will not be judged. Do not condemn, and you will not be condemned. Forgive, and you will be forgiven." (Luke 6:37 NIV)

Lead us not into temptation but deliver us from evil

Pray for protection from evil. Pray for God's help and protection from sin and temptation:

> 'Finally, be strong in the Lord and in his mighty power. Put on the full armour of God, so that you can take your stand against the devil's schemes. For our struggle is not against flesh and blood, but against the rulers, against the authorities, against the powers of this dark world and against the spiritual forces of evil in the heavenly realms. Therefore put on the full armour of God, so that when the day of evil comes, you may be able to stand your ground, and after

Jesus' Pattern for Prayer

you have done everything, to stand. Stand firm then, with the belt of truth buckled around your waist, with the breastplate of righteousness in place, and with your feet fitted with the readiness that comes from the gospel of peace. In addition to all this, take up the shield of faith, with which you can extinguish all the flaming arrows of the evil one. Take the helmet of salvation and the sword of the Spirit, which is the word of God.' (Ephesians 6:10-17 NIV)

Remind yourself God has the power to do far more than you can imagine.

Pray for all things to be done to God's glory and believe that God is faithful to answer your prayers.

Pray this prayer.....

Lord Jesus, please help me to follow your example of prayer, I thank you for all you are doing in my life and I avail myself to be used by you for the
advancement of your kingdom. Amen

4

Praying with Authority

I always say that God cannot do anymore than He has done. He sent Jesus to earth, who died on the cross for us and He rose from the dead to give us eternal life. In his death, he took back the keys of authority that had been handed over to the enemy by our sin, as stated in the book of Revelation 1:18 -

> "I am the Living One; I was dead, and now look, I am alive for ever and ever!
> And I hold the keys of death and Hades."

Jesus passes on those keys to His church, you and me! We are Christ's legal power of attorney here on earth, we act on His behalf, with His authority He has given us. So, when we pray, we must pray with authority and with faith.

Matt 16:18-19 (KJV) tells us

> "And I say also unto thee, That thou art Peter, and upon this rock I will build my church; and the gates of hell shall

not prevail against it.
And I will give unto thee the keys of the kingdom of heaven: and whatsoever thou shalt bind on earth shall be bound in heaven: and whatsoever thou shalt loose on earth shall be loosed in heaven."

But, having the keys and using the keys are two different things. This reminds me of a healing meeting I attended with my late husband Stuart Lovejoy, about 30 years ago. It was a meeting put on by a tremendous man of God called John Wimber at the Royal Albert Hall.

I was in awe of how this man of God would call forth healings to a room full of hundreds of people, located at different places in the room. As the meeting progressed, he asked us to get into groups of four to six people to pray for each other. Stuart and I got into our group and we took turns to pray and when it was the turn of a lady in our group to pray, she said - 'Satan please can you leave us alone and stop troubling my family.'

You can imagine the shock in me and my husband's ears hearing this. Stuart looked at me and interjected and said, 'Can I just stop you a moment - we do not ask Satan to leave us, we tell him! We have authority over him because of what Christ did for us. We then prayed again as a group commanding the devil to flee and stop troubling the lady.

The point I want to make is that this precious lady did not know how to use the keys of authority or faith that God availed to us by Christ. However, after we prayed with her, showing her how to pray and explained the authority she has in Christ as a believer, she did understand and thanked us for explaining it to her.

So, when we pray, we must be tenacious and pray with the authority that we have.

The bible tells of different people who prayed and exercised their faith and authority. One such person was Elijah. He was a great man who prayed earnestly and demonstrated the supernatural power of prayer.

Throughout the chapter of 1 Kings 17 in the bible, we read where Elijah told King Ahab there would be no rain, and it didn't rain for three years.

God wants us to pray from a position of declaration and authority over things in our lives and what He directs us to pray about. After all, He has seated us in heavenly places with Christ Jesus:

'And God raised us up with Christ and seated us with Him in the heavenly realms in Christ Jesus.' (Ephesians 2:6 NIV)

Jesus has also given us as believers, authority over all the power of the enemy:

'Then he called his twelve disciples together, and gave them power and authority over all devils, and to cure diseases. And he sent them to preach the kingdom of God, and to heal the sick.' (Luke 9:1-2 NIV)

Pray this prayer.....

I exalt you Lord and thank you for your loving kindness and that your mercies are new every morning. Thank you for your blood which washes away my sin and covers me and all pertaining to my life. I decree and declare in the mighty Name of Jesus Christ of Nazareth that no unclean

Praying with Authority

spirit is welcome in my life and take authority and cast out anything contrary to Jesus my Lord and Saviour, in my life. I thank you for the victory and that you always cause me to triumph. Amen

5

The Holy Spirit and Prayer

The Holy Spirit is the third person of the Trinity - Father, Son and the Holy Spirit. The Holy Spirit carries the presence of God and His power.

1 John 5:7 (KJV) reads: *'For there are three that bear record in heaven, the Father, the Word, and the Holy Ghost: and these three are one.'*

The Father is the Almighty God, The Son is our Lord Jesus Christ, and The Holy Spirit is the One who Jesus sent to us.

It is imperative as a believer in Christ that we allow the Holy Spirit to be part of our prayer life. God is the power source through the Holy Spirit for us to walk in authority to act.

Having the Holy Spirit in our lives and prayer life will awaken our abilities. He will communicate His power, He will bring us into the realm of power, will transmit His divine power through us and guide us into all truth.

The Holy Spirit will guide you and direct you how to pray. Jesus promised to send the Holy Spirit to us, as evidenced in John 14:16-17 (ESV):

"I will ask the Father, and He will give you another Helper, that He may be with you forever; that is the Spirit of truth, whom the world cannot receive, because it does not see Him or know Him, but you know Him because He abides with you and will be in you."

The more we open ourselves to the Holy Spirit when we pray, the more we will see Christ-like behaviour traits that are representative of Jesus. In the book of Galatians, Paul refers to these characteristics as the fruit of the Spirit which is love, joy, peace, patience, kindness, goodness, faithfulness, and self-control (Galatians 5:22-23 KJV).

The Holy Spirit forms the indwelling Christ in our hearts and minds. Paul prays this for the Ephesians -

'For this reason I bow my knees before the Father, from whom every family in heaven and on earth is named, that according to the riches of his glory he may grant you to be strengthened with power through his Spirit in your inner being, so that Christ may dwell in your hearts through faith—that you, being rooted and grounded in love, may have strength to comprehend with all the saints what is the breadth and length and height and depth, and to know the love of Christ that surpasses knowledge, that you may be filled with all the fullness of God.

Now to him who is able to do far more abundantly than all that we ask or think, according to the power at work within us, to him be glory in the church and in Christ Jesus throughout all generations, forever and ever. Amen.' (Eph. 3:14-21 NIV)

Through the indwelling of the Holy Spirit within us, we also have the spirit of Christ dwelling in our inner man. God wants us to have the Spirit of His Son in us, and why we need the Holy Spirit to help us in prayer, is because Jesus was and is our model for prayer.

The Holy Spirit intercedes for us

When we pray the Holy Spirit intercedes for us on earth to makes our prayers acceptable to God. We are then able to pray according to God's will and be conformed to the image of Jesus:

> 'For those God foreknew he also predestined to be conformed to the image of his Son, that he might be the firstborn among many brothers and sisters' (Romans 8:29 NIV)

The Holy Spirit helps us to wait with patience

We read in Romans that we groan within, awaiting our redemption and the Holy Spirit feels our groans and He makes intercessions for us. This helps us to pray whilst we await our redemption -

> 'Not only so, but we ourselves, who have the firstfruits of the Spirit, groan inwardly as we wait eagerly for our adoption to sonship, the redemption of our bodies. For in this hope we were saved. But hope that is seen is no hope at all. Who hopes for what they already have? But if we hope for

what we do not yet have, we wait for it patiently. In the same way, the Spirit helps us in our weakness. We do not know what we ought to pray for, but the Spirit himself intercedes for us through wordless groans' (Romans 8:23-26 NIV).

Through the Holy Spirit's intercession, He helps us to pray that we would wait patiently, for our redemption and that we spend our time wisely, not living a sinful life but according to His Spirit, and according to how Jesus would live.

The book of Titus sums it up well for us -

'For the grace of God has appeared, bringing salvation to everyone. It instructs us to renounce ungodliness and worldly passions, and to live sensible, upright, and godly lives in the present age, as we await the blessed hope and glorious appearance of our great God and Savior Jesus Christ....' (Titus 2:11-13 NIV).

The Holy Spirit burdens us and guides us in prayer

The Holy Spirit helps and encourages us in prayer by placing a prayer burden on us. It could be having someone placed on your heart and you feel led to pray for them, or over a specific situation.

The Holy Spirit burdens us by transferring God's burden to us as we pray and live in the Spirit. The result is that we groan in prayer with the same burden and this also guides us in what to pray for. He will inspire us with words to express our prayer thoughts and also helps to recall scriptural promises that come from the heart of God, our heavenly Father:

> 'In the same way, the Spirit helps us in our weakness. We do not know what we ought to pray for, but the Spirit himself intercedes for us through wordless groans. And he who searches our hearts knows the mind of the Spirit, because the Spirit intercedes for God's people in accordance with the will of God' (Romans 8:26-27 NIV)

The Holy Spirit teaches and strengthens us in prayer

The Holy Spirit will teach you many things in your prayer walk. He will teach you how to know His prompting, direction on what to pray for and will speak to you through things that resonate with you. If you have no strength, faith or desire to pray, He will strengthen you if you ask Him to. I remember when my late husband Stuart died unexpectedly, I was broken in my spirit. It was a very emotive time for me. I can honestly say, only God carried. In addition, the Holy Spirit would whisper scriptures into my soul to get me through and give me the words to speak so I could find the strength to get through the day and the words to pray in that season of my life. He will do the same for you if you feel weak in spirit.

In the book of 1 John 5:14-15 (NIV) it tells us:

> 'This is the confidence we have in approaching God: that if we ask anything according to his will, he hears us. And if we know that he hears us - whatever we ask - we know

that we have what we asked of him.'

He will strengthen us as we pray and our faith will grow as well.

The Holy Spirit is our advocate before God when we pray

The Holy Spirit helps us to pray and when He dwells in us, guarantees answers to our prayers and advocates for us before God -

> 'But you, dear friends, by building yourselves up in your most holy faith and praying in the Holy Spirit....' (Jude 1:20 NIV).

Pray this prayer .....

Holy Spirit of the living God, come and dwell in me. Wash me with the renewing of my mind with the word of God, dwell in me I pray. Let me be baptised by you with evidence of speaking in tongues and guided by you in all truth. Amen

6

Types of Prayer

In this chapter we will look at some of the different types of prayers that are prayed.

The bible tells us in the book of James 5:16 (AMP) that 'The earnest (insistent, fervent, heartfelt, continued) prayer of a righteous person achieves much (is powerfully effective)'.

There are diverse prayers for different occasions and for specific needs.

Prayer of supplication

This type of prayer is when we entreat God to intervene on our behalf and request something -

> 'Be anxious for nothing, but in everything by prayer and supplication, with thanksgiving, let your requests be made known to God' (Philippians 4:6 NIV).

Prayer of intercession

Intercessory prayer is praying to God on behalf of someone -

'So I sought for a man among them who would make a wall, and stand in the gap before Me on behalf of the land, that I should not destroy it; but I found no one' (Ezekiel 22:30).

'Therefore I exhort first of all that supplications, prayers, intercessions, and giving of thanks be made for all men' (1 Timothy 2:1 KJV).

Prayer of faith

This type of prayer is calling on the Elders in your church family or body of Christ to collectively stand with you for a prayer need you have -*'Is anyone among you suffering? Let him pray. Is anyone cheerful? Let him sing psalms. Is anyone among you sick? Let him call for the elders of the church, and let them pray over him, anointing him with oil in the name of the Lord. And the prayer of faith will save the sick, and the Lord will raise him up. And if he has committed sins, he will be forgiven'* (James 5:13-15 KJV).

Corporate prayer

Corporate praying happens when we pray together as the body of Christ in agreement -

'These all continued with one accord in prayer and supplication, with the women and Mary the mother of Jesus, and with His brothers' (Acts 1:14 KJV).

And they continued steadfastly in the apostles' doctrine and fellowship, in the breaking of bread, and in prayers' (Acts 2:42 KJV).

Praying in the spirit or praying in tongues

This type of prayer is praying as the Holy Spirit guides you, so ultimately praying according to the will of God -

'For he who speaks in a tongue does not speak to men but to God, for no one understands him; however, in the spirit he speaks mysteries' (1 Corinthians 14:2).

'For if I pray in a tongue, my spirit prays, but my understanding is unfruitful. What is the conclusion then? I will pray with the spirit, and I will also pray with the understanding. I will sing with the spirit, and I will also sing with the understanding' (1 Corinthians 14:14-15 KJV).

'Likewise, the Spirit also helps in our weaknesses. For we do not know what we should pray for as we ought, but the Spirit Himself makes intercession for us with groanings which cannot be uttered' (Romans 8:26 KJV).

Types of Prayer

Prayer of thanksgiving

Thanksgiving prayers acknowledge God's goodness in our lives and offering praise to Him for it -

'Enter into His gates with thanksgiving, And into His courts with praise. Be thankful to Him, and bless His name' (Psalm 100:4 KJV).

Prayer of confession and repentance

This type of prayer is seeking forgiveness from God for our wrong-doing and repenting from our sins, just as we did when we asked Jesus into our lives and confessed Him as Lord and Saviour -

'If we confess our sins, He is faithful and just to forgive us our sins and to cleanse us from all unrighteousness' (1 John 1:9 KJV).

'Confess your trespasses to one another, and pray for one another, that you may be healed. The effective, fervent prayer of a righteous man avails much' (James 5:16 KJV).

Prayer of dedication or consecration

This type of prayer is when we give our all to God and avail ourselves to be used by Him for His kingdom –

'Then Joshua said to the people, "Consecrate yourselves, for tomorrow the LORD will do wonders among you" ' (Joshua 3:5 ESV)

'He went a little farther and fell on His face, and prayed, saying, "O My Father, if it is possible, let this cup pass from Me; nevertheless, not as I will, but as You will" ' (Matthew 26:39 KJV).

'Then Samson called to the Lord, saying, "O Lord God, remember me, I pray! Strengthen me, I pray, just this once, O God, that I may with one blow take vengeance on the Philistines for my two eyes!" ' (Judges 16:28 KJV).

The Lord's prayer

This prayer is stated in Matthew 6 and it shows a model of how believers should pray to God as covered in detail in chapter 3.

Prayer of agreement

This type of prayer is an exercise of spiritual authority as led by the Holy Spirit and being in complete harmony with one another and with the Lord. It is a joint level of spiritual faith and agreement that whatever is being believed for will be manifested from the spiritual realm into the natural. In this type of prayer, two or more believers are in agreement for the specific thing being prayed for -

Types of Prayer

'Again I say unto you, That if two of you shall agree on earth as touching anything that they shall ask, it shall be done for them of my Father which is in heaven' (Matthew 18:19 KJV).

Prayer to move mountains

Mountain-moving prayer is used to address obstacles, problems, or circumstances that seem like mountains to you in your life and require you to use your measure of faith to believe for answers to your prayers -

' "Truly I tell you, if you have faith as small as a mustard seed, you can say to this mountain, 'Move from here to there,' and it will move. Nothing will be impossible for you" ' (Matthew 18:19 KJV).

Memorial prayer

In the book of Acts we read about a centurion called Cornelius who activated his faith by giving offerings, his prayers ascended as a memorial before God. The prayer of faith is powerful and giving offerings to the Lord is powerful. It's like igniting a fire to cause an explosion of faith to be released.

The key with memorial prayer is to construct your prayer, and give an offering to God or make a solemn promise to God. This is a tool to help release your faith to God at the time of prayer - *'One day at about the ninth hour, he had a clear vision of an angel of God who came to him and said, "Cornelius!" Cornelius stared at him in fear and asked, "What is it, Lord?" The angel answered, "Your prayers and gifts to the poor have ascended as a memorial offering before God"* ' (Acts 10:4 NKJV).

Pray this prayer .....

> Lord help me to pray and to be open to the leading and prompting of your Holy Spirit. I pray I always check the motive behind my prayers and actions and ask you to guide me and pray for your perfect will in my life. Amen

7

Angels and Prayer

Angels take a proactive part in our prayer life. In no way are we ever to worship them or pray to them. God has given us angels to help us here in the natural realm and to also help manifest answers to our prayer petitions from the spiritual realm as directed by God.

I remember in 2005 I had pressing financial bills which led me to pray and pray and pray! I went to church on the Sunday and during the worship I saw an angel literally descend from heaven and he looked at me and came over to me and said these exact words:

'I come to give you a word of encouragement, not a word of woe.
God has heard your prayer and within three days
He will answer your prayer.
Now begin to praise God!'

With that he turned and walked to the spot from which he had appeared and went back up to heaven.

Well, we were worshipping in church at that moment and I did indeed praise God for His kindness and grace to send an angel to me, of all people.

The story does not end there. A good friend of ours who we had not heard from for a good few months phoned me and said, 'God told me to ring you. He told me that you need money. How much do you need?' I told him we needed £600 to pay bills and he sent the money. And just as the angel had said, it was within three days, in fact on the third day!

I shared the testimony with this friend and he was blown away by it all and delighted God used him.

Why I share this with you is to show you how angels are used by God to help us and to show you the role angels play in your prayers. In the book of Revelation chapter 8, John tells us about what happens concerning the prayers of the saints:

> 'Then another angel, who had a golden censer, came and stood at the altar. He was given much incense to offer, along with the prayers of all the saints, on the golden altar before the throne. The smoke of the incense, together with the prayers of the saints, rose up before God from the hand of the angel' (Rev 8:3-4 NKJV).

This verse tells us that the smoke from the burning incense included the prayers of the saints! How exciting is that? Our prayer rises up to God - that's you and me.

God loves hearing our prayers, in fact He delights in the prayers of His saints.

1 Peter 3:12 says, *'The eyes of the Lord are on the righteous, and his ears are open to their prayer.'*

Be encouraged to know our prayers please God. In the book of Hebrews, He invites us to draw near to His throne with confidence, *'that we may receive mercy and find grace to help in time of need'* (Hebrews 4:16).

So, be comforted with the thought that when you pray, God hears you and your prayers are hand-delivered by an angel, purified with much incense before the throne of God. And that is *all* your prayers. We serve a wonderful God who will perfect that which concerns us (Psalm 138:8).

Pray this prayer .....

Lord, thank you for every single gift you have given us and thank you for your angels and what they do for us. Lord, help me to have my ears, eyes and heart open to you and to step out in faith and understanding as you lead me. Amen

7

Prayer

Prayer is a privilege. We have direct access to Him but sometimes if answers are delayed, we doubt ourselves; we doubt God and question everything that we believe.

We can feel like our prayers are going no further than the ceiling. In our most troubled times in life when we are going through trials, the feeling can be intensified, but be assured, God does hear you.

There are a few reasons why prayers appear not to be answered. God is sovereign and sometimes He delays the answer to pray for the correct time, in order to protect you.

There are some prayers that with hindsight I am so grateful that God did not answer for me when I have passed through a season and saw that what I thought would be a good fit, would have been a nightmare.

Here are some reasons why prayers aren't answered -

Prayer

We don't ask God for help or a solution

I know this sounds a bit obvious, but sometimes we allow situations to overwhelm us, then sit in the rocking chair of worry, going back and forth going nowhere, whine, cry our tears.

We strive to fix things in our strength and guess what, it does not work until you pray and then things begin to shift.

James 4:2 says, *'You desire but do not have, so you kill. You covet but you cannot get what you want, so you quarrel and fight. You do not have because you do not ask God.'*

We need to check our motive when we pray

The book of James 4:3 says, *'And when you do ask, you do not receive, because you ask with wrong motives, that you may squander it on your pleasures.'* When we pray we must check our motive as to why we are praying for this outcome or a particular thing.

God sees our heart and the motive in it. Our motives are never hidden from him. *"I the Lord search the heart and test the mind, to give every man according to his ways, according to the fruit of his deeds."* (Jeremiah 17:10 KJV).

If we have unconfessed sin in our life

We are sinners redeemed by grace. We need to acknowledge our shortcomings, confess our sins. We need to face up to sin in our life, not rationalise it. It will hinder your walk with God and rob you of your faith and anointing when you pray.

Romans 3:23 (KJV) instructs us –*'for all have sinned and fall* short of the glory of God.'

1 John 1:9 (NLT) says, *'But if we confess our sins to him, he is faithful and just to forgive us our sins and to cleanse us from all wickedness.'*

God's mercy is new every morning. He is faithful and just to forgive us of our sins once we confess them to him. If we don't seek his forgiveness, it will cause spiritual blocks in our lives and hinder our prayers from being answered.

We pray soulish prayers outside of God's will

We can pray till the cows come home over something so hard, pull out all the spiritual know-hows and still, nothing. We pray with our own agenda and do not take into account God's will in the situation.

1 John 5:14-15 (NLT) reminds us, *'And we are confident that he hears us whenever we ask for anything that pleases him. And since we know he hears us when we make our requests, we also know that he will give us what we ask for.'*

When we pray we need to check we are praying God's will and not soulish wishy- washy desires that are not His. When we pray with a prideful spirit

Matthew 6:5 (KJV) advises -

'When you pray, don't be like the hypocrites who love to pray publicly on street corners and in the synagogues where everyone can see them. I tell you the truth, that is all the reward they will ever get.'

Jesus called out the Pharisees of His day for their hypocritical behaviour when they prayed, being religious and wanting

Prayer

everyone to see how holy they were.

If we pray with pride, those prayers don't get answered. A prideful spirit becomes an unteachable one. We must be humble before the Lord and He will exalt us.

Pride focuses on self, as in what we have done, while humility focuses on God and what He can do. That's the difference.

Say this prayer .....

Lord, teach me to be open to you and your ways and when I pray, I ask that you hear me. I pray for your forgiveness if I have done anything to hinder my relationship with you, cleanse me I ask. I pray I walk in your ways always. Amen

Answered Prayer

In this chapter I want to share with you, testimonies of answered prayers of everyday people like you and me and people from the bible.

If we truly believe and know Christ, we have a guarantee because of His righteousness, that we are made righteous and that answered prayer is not only possible, but it is also assured to the righteous.

In the book of James 5:16 (NLT)it tells us -

'The earnest prayer of a righteous person has great power and wonderful results".

We can have confidence that God will hear us and answer us!

We are reminded in 1 John 5:14-15 (ESV), *'And this is the confidence that we have toward him, that if we ask anything according to his will he hears us. And if we know that he hears us in whatever we ask, we know that we have the requests that we have asked of him.'*

Answered Prayer

The bible is full of lots of scriptures about prayer and true-life events where God answered prayers.

I am in no way religious, I don't spend seven hours a day praying, but I am in constant communication with God. I do pray and talk to Him throughout the day and stay in the secret place. Incidentally, whilst writing this book at this very moment, my pet tortoise that I put out in the garden in an enclosure, escaped! I had to stop writing and go out and look for her. We searched everywhere; we could not see her. My dog, Buddy, kept barking at a certain area of the garden we had already checked, but we still could not see her. I prayed and smiled at the irony that I was writing about prayer being answered and asked the Holy Spirit to show me where this little tortoise was. Once again, Buddy barked at the same spot we had previously looked at and guess what, we dug deeper in the heap of leaves and found her. I was so relieved. God truly does answer prayer.

I wish to encourage you and share prayers God has answered for me and others. God is no respecter of person and will answer you too.

Here is one of the quickest answers I received:

When I was 19 years old, I loved to invite everyone over for dinner and I remember I was short on cash. I prayed a simple prayer, saying, 'Lord, I would like £30 to buy stuff to make dinner for my friends and also to have some money for my offering on Sunday. Amen.'

No sooner had I said 'Amen', the phone rang and it was my pastor's wife, Angela (who is one of my dearest friends today) and she asked if she could buy a spare bed that I had, for her son, for £30! Of course, I said yes and told her God used her to answer my prayer.

I haven't got a clue Lord but you have! ......

My lovely friend, Melanie Jackson, shared this testimony with me about God's healing power. Whilst on a mission trip in Africa, Melanie, prayed a simple prayer when directed by the preacher in the meeting she was attending.

Mel was new to this and felt her heart flutter, but got the courage to give it a go. Standing in front of her was a lady whose arms were outstretched to heaven with faith and praising God. Melanie, simply put her hand on her belly and prayed, 'I have not got a clue what this lady needs but you have, Lord.' She immediately felt a popping movement on her hands, which freaked her out. The lady meanwhile is ecstatic with joy, praising God. Mel called for an interpreter to ask her what happened and the lady said she had a hernia which was now completely healed! Praise God.

Prayer for Tinnitus

Patrick had been suffering with tinnitus for three months and asked Melanie to pray for him. They were at a conference and in faith Melanie went into the kitchen and grabbed some cooking oil and asked those in the kitchen at the time to pray for fire on her hands. She walked over to Patrick, placed her hands on his ears and before she even prayed, he declared, 'It's gone!'

God will meet you at your point of need and faith level. He is just and faithful, shows mercy and love to His children.

Buddy the Beagle - praying him in

I had a beautiful black labrador called Joshua, who died. My family and I were heartbroken and then decided we wanted another dog when we felt ready, but wanted a Beagle and also wanted our next dog to be a 'rescue'. We prayed and asked God to direct us, went to dog shelters and also looked on the internet. Eventually, my daughter found a Beagle that needed rehoming on *Preloved Pets*. I immediately responded to their advert and within two days Buddy arrived to live with us. He is a blessing.

I have endless testimonies of God's continued answers to prayer in my life. He is faithful. And now we can look at a few people from the bible who prayed and God answered them.

Hezekiah

In the book of 2 Kings 20, we read the story of Hezekiah who was sick and at death's door and God sent His prophet Isaiah to inform him of his impending death.

Here was a prophet of God sent directly to inform him to put his house in order and be prepared to die.

Hezekiah did not waste any time and prayed and reminded God of how he had walked with Him in his youth. God answered Hezekiah's prayer and sent the prophet to tell him He had added fifteen years to his life. It just shows you God's promise to answer us whenever we call.

"It shall come to pass That before they call, I will answer; And while they are still speaking, I will hear" (Isaiah 65:24 KJV).

Hezekiah didn't indulge in self-pity when he received news of his death date. Instead, he quickly humbled himself before God and prayed.

Hannah

1 Samuel chapter one introduces us to Hannah, who was childless in a polygamous marriage. She lived in a tense household, as the other wife, her rival, had many children. Despite this, Hannah would always go yearly to the house of the Lord and pray.

She promised God that if He blessed her with a child, she would give the child back to Him to be used. That child would later become the prophet, Samuel. Hannah was blessed with five additional children.

The Church, when Peter was imprisoned

The account in Acts 12 is an outstanding example of answered prayer. It's an account of how King Herod arrested Peter and put him in prison to please the Jews. He had previously ordered the killing of James and since it pleased the Jews, he proceeded to take Peter.

Something different happened however, because the church offered continuous prayer (v5) to God for him. The incessant prayers reached God's throne room and He sent His angel to miraculously rescue Peter from the prison where he was bound in chains between two soldiers. It was a miracle because the soldiers to whom he was bound on either side, didn't realise

Answered Prayer

until daybreak, that Peter was gone.

9

Prayers you can use to pray

Salvation prayer

Lord Jesus, I confess my sins and ask for your forgiveness. Please come into my heart as my Lord and Saviour. Take complete control of my life and help me to walk in your footsteps daily, by the power of the Holy Spirit. Thank you, Lord, for saving me and for answering my prayer. Amen.

Finances

Dear God, your word says that you will supply all our needs according to your riches in glory by Christ Jesus and I believe in what you said. Your word does not return void, so if your word says it, you will do it. Amen

Prayers you can use to pray

Prayer covering over family members

Dear Lord, I'm calling on you to help my children. They're young and afraid and fearful of what they see happening in the world around them. May your strength and power rest on my children. Comfort them during this time of fear and confusion. Give them the strength to live each day with peace and confidence. In 1 Peter 5:7 you tell us, *'Cast all your anxiety on him because he cares for you.'* We are trusting in the power of your words and resting in the fact that you truly care for us.

Prayer of spiritual protection over yourself

Dear Lord, in the name of Jesus Christ of Nazareth, I declare that I am your anointed. I declare all ill-spoken words against my life to become null and void. I shall not be overtaken by the lips of talkers. I cancel the malicious words of talkers, their gossip has no power over me and shall be exposed, in Jesus mighty Name.
Everyone bearing false witness against me shall be overthrown and exposed, in Jesus mighty Name. All enemies who pretend to be my friends but are friendly enemies and backstabbers shall be overthrown, in Jesus Name.
Every meeting in the secret places, in the den of occultists, and groves of witches where I, my affairs, my business, family and Church are being discussed, the power of God shall scatter their words and counsel and make them of no

effect.

I cancel every curse, hex, rumour, lie and divination. Enchantments being spoken over me shall not overtake my destiny. I am immune to all negative words and ill-spoken words. They have no effect over my life, my household and my destiny. Tongues are weapons, and so all tongues that are speaking against me negatively, to reduce my influence and my blessing, shall not prosper. They shall not prosper today, not tomorrow and not forever, in Jesus mighty Name.

Prayer of protection for travelling and covering in the midst of the storm

Psalm 91- Pray it over yourself and loved ones:

> 'He who dwells in the shelter of the Most High will abide in the shadow of the Almighty. I will say to the Lord, "My refuge and my fortress, my God, in whom I trust."
> For he will deliver you from the snare of the fowler and from the deadly pestilence. He will cover you with his pinions, and under his wings you will find refuge; his faithfulness is a shield and buckler. You will not fear the terror of the night, nor the arrow that flies by day, nor the pestilence that stalks in darkness, nor the destruction that wastes at noonday.
> A thousand may fall at your side, ten thousand at your right hand, but it will not come near you. You will only look with your eyes and see the recompense of the wicked. Because you have made the Lord your dwelling place - the

Prayers you can use to pray

Most High, who is my refuge - no evil shall be allowed to befall you, no plague come near your tent. For he will command his angels concerning you to guard you in all your ways. On their hands they will bear you up, lest you strike your foot against a stone. You will tread on the lion and the adder; the young lion and the serpent you will trample underfoot. "Because he holds fast to me in love, I will deliver him; I will protect him, because he knows my name. When he calls to me, I will answer him; I will be with him in trouble; I will rescue him and honour him. With long life I will satisfy him and show him my salvation.'" (Psalm 91 ESV)

Deliverance prayer

In the name of JESUS, I cover myself and the one reading this with the Blood of JESUS. I ask for giant warrior angels to protect us. As your war club and weapons of war, I break down, undam, and blow up all walls of protection around all witches, warlocks, wizards, satanists, sorcerers, and the like, and I break the power of all curses, hexes, vexes, spells, charms, fetishes, psychic prayers, psychic thoughts, all witchcraft, sorcery, magic, voodoo, all mind control, jinxes, potions, bewitchments, death, destruction, sickness, pain, torment, psychic power, psychic warfare, prayer chains, incense and candle burning, incantations, chanting, blessings, hoodoo, crystals, root works, and everything else being sent my way, or my family member's way, or any Deliverance Ministries way, and I return it, and the demons to the sender, SEVENFOLD, and I bind it to them by the Blood of Jesus, and I cut and burn their ungodly silver cords and lay-lines, in JESUS' Name.

(Prayer from demonbuster.com)

10

Answered Prayer record log pages

Your prayer record

Write your prayer request here

Date

And write here how God answered your prayer, don't forget to date it.

God Answers Prayer

Your prayer record

Write your prayer request here

Date

And write here how God answered your prayer, don't forget to date it.

Answered Prayer record log pages

Your prayer record

Write your prayer request here

Date

And write here how God answered your prayer, don't forget to date it.

God Answers Prayer

Your prayer record

Write your prayer request here

Date

And write here how God answered your prayer, don't forget to date it.

Answered Prayer record log pages

Your prayer record

Write your prayer request here

Date

And write here how God answered your prayer, don't forget to date it.

Your prayer record

Write your prayer request here

Date

And write here how God answered your prayer, don't forget to date it.

Answered Prayer record log pages

Your prayer record

Write your prayer request here

Date

And write here how God answered your prayer, don't forget to date it.

God Answers Prayer

Your prayer record

Write your prayer request here

Date

And write here how God answered your prayer, don't forget to date it.

www.ingramcontent.com/pod-product-compliance
Lightning Source LLC
Chambersburg PA
CBHW050447010526
44118CB00013B/1716